BRITANNICA BEGINNER BIOS

FREDERICK DOUGLASS

ABOLITIONIST AND FIGHTER FOR EQUALITY

JASON PORTERFIELD

Britannica Educational Publishing
IN ASSOCIATION WITH
ROSEN
EDUCATIONAL SERVICES

Published in 2018 by Britannica Educational Publishing (a trademark of Encyclopædia Britannica, Inc.) in association with The Rosen Publishing Group, Inc.
29 East 21st Street, New York, NY 10010

Distributed exclusively by Rosen Publishing.
To see additional Britannica Educational Publishing titles, go to rosenpublishing.com.

First Edition

Britannica Educational Publishing
J.E. Luebering: Executive Director, Core Editorial
Mary Rose McCudden: Editor, Britannica Student Encyclopedia

Rosen Publishing
Kathy Kuhtz Campbell: Senior Editor
Nelson Sá: Art Director
Brian Garvey: Series Designer
Ellina Litmanovich: Book Layout
Cindy Reiman: Photography Manager
Bruce Donnola: Photo Researcher

Library of Congress Cataloging-in-Publication Data

Names: Porterfield, Jason, author.
Title: Frederick Douglass: abolitionist and fighter for equality / Jason Porterfield.
Description: New York: Britannica Educational Publishing, in Association with Rosen Educational Services, 2018 | Series: Britannica beginner bios | Includes bibliographical references and index. | Audience: Grades 1–4.
Identifiers: LCCN 2017015307| ISBN 9781680488036 (library bound: alk. paper) | ISBN 9781680488029 (pbk.: alk. paper) | ISBN 9781538300190 (6 pack: alk. paper)
Subjects: LCSH: Douglass, Frederick, 1818–1895—Juvenile literature. | Slaves—United States—Biography––Juvenile literature. | Abolitionists—United States—Biography—Juvenile literature. | African American abolitionists—Biography—Juvenile literature. | Antislavery movements—United States—History—Juvenile literature. | African Americans—History—19th century—Juvenile literature.
Classification: LCC E449.D75 P67 2018 | DDC 973.8092 [B] —dc23
LC record available at https://lccn.loc.gov/2017015307

Manufactured in the United States of America

Photo credits: Cover, p. 1 American School/Getty Images; pp. 5, 6 Encyclopædia Britannica, Inc.; pp. 7, 24 © North Wind Picture Archives; pp. 9, 15, 21, 22, 25 Library of Congress Prints and Photographs Division; p. 10 Three Lions/Hulton Archive/Getty Images; p. 11 Fotosearch/Archive Photos/Getty Images; pp. 13, 19 Hulton Archive/Getty Images; p. 14 Private Collection/Bridgeman Images; p. 16 Culture Club/Hulton Archive/Getty Images; p. 17 Massachusetts Historical Society, Boston, MA, USA/Bridgeman Images; pp. 27, 28 The Washington Post/Getty Images.

CONTENTS

CHAPTER ONE

INTRODUCING FREDERICK DOUGLASS

Frederick Douglass was a brilliant writer and speaker who lived during the nineteenth century. He was also a former slave and a leader of the movement to end slavery. Slavery is the practice of people owning other people. The people who are enslaved are forced to work without pay. Slavery was common in many parts of the United States until the middle of the 1860s. American slaves were people who had been stolen from Africa and their **DESCENDANTS**.

Douglass was an educated slave at a time when it was illegal for slaves to know how to read and write. After he escaped from slavery, he used his education to give speeches and to write about the horrors of

Vocabulary

DESCENDANTS are people who are related to a person or group of people who lived in the past.

slavery. His words helped to turn many white Americans against slavery. He spoke to large crowds across the northern and midwestern United States. He even traveled to Europe to give speeches.

After slavery ended, Douglass continued to work for the rights of African

Frederick Douglass was one of the most famous leaders of the fight to end slavery in the United States.

Quick Fact

Douglass earned the money to start his first newspaper by giving speeches in Europe.

Americans. His work inspired many African Americans. He showed people that it was possible to escape from slavery and become successful. His life also gave proof to white people that African Americans had the ability to succeed.

The Underground Railroad was a secret network of routes and hideouts that escaped slaves used to make it to the northern states.

Douglass went on a speaking tour of Great Britain and Ireland, where he impressed many people with his speeches about his time in slavery.

Douglass also supported women's rights. He was active in the fight to give women the right to vote.

Later in life, Douglass held many important government jobs. He was a pioneer because no other African American had held those jobs before. He also continued to write, publish newspapers, and give speeches. Today, his speeches and books still have the power to inspire people.

CHAPTER TWO

BORN INTO SLAVERY

No one knows exactly when Frederick Douglass was born. He was born into slavery, and slaveholders seldom recorded the exact dates that slaves were born. It is believed that he was born in the year 1818 in Talbot County, Maryland. His birth name was Frederick Augustus Washington Bailey. He changed his name after he escaped from slavery.

Quick Fact

When he was older, Frederick always celebrated his birthday on February 14.

Frederick's mother, Harriet Bailey, was an African American slave. The only thing Frederick knew of his father was that he was a white man. Since his mother was a slave, Frederick was also a slave. He was separated from his mother while he was still an infant, and he lived with his grandmother on a Maryland **PLANTATION**. Frederick also had a brother and two sisters, but slavery kept them apart for many years.

Vocabulary

In the early United States, a PLANTATION was a large farm worked by slaves.

Frederick saw his mother

Frederick spent part of his childhood living with his grandmother at the Wye House Plantation in rural Talbot County, Maryland.

very little and had only a few memories of her from his childhood. She died when he was about seven years old.

When he was about eight years old, Frederick was sent to live in the city of Baltimore, Maryland. He became a house servant for the family of a man named Hugh Auld.

Working in the Auld home changed Frederick's life. Hugh Auld's wife, Sophia, taught Frederick how to

Young slaves like Frederick were often given jobs in and around the plantation house until they were old enough to work in the fields.

Because it was illegal in many places for slaves to learn how to read, most did not get the chance to learn unless they were freed.

read and write, even though it was illegal to educate slaves in Maryland.

Hugh Auld learned about the lessons and stopped them. He believed that education would make Frederick unfit for being a slave. However, Frederick had already learned the alphabet and some basic words. He was able to get some white children who lived nearby to teach him more. He read newspapers and books whenever he could get them.

CHAPTER THREE

GAINING FREEDOM

Reading opened Frederick up to new ideas. He read a book of speeches against slavery. The speeches made his hatred of slavery grow. They also inspired him to work to end slavery, even though he was still a slave.

In 1832, Frederick was sent away from the Auld home in Baltimore. He went to work on a plantation owned by Hugh Auld's brother, Thomas. Frederick became a field slave and was treated more harshly than before. Slaves who worked inside were often better fed and given better clothes than those who worked in the field. Field slaves had to work outside from morning to night in all kinds of weather.

Slaves had to do the hardest jobs on a plantation, including harvesting, planting, and compressing cotton. They had very little time to themselves.

Thomas Auld thought that Frederick had too much pride. He put Frederick in the hands of a "slave breaker" named Edward Covey. Covey beat Frederick harshly over many months. One day, Frederick and Covey fought and Frederick won. He later saw the fight as a turning point in his life because he stood up for himself.

In 1834, Frederick was then sent to another plantation owned by a man named William Freeland. Freeland was kinder than Thomas Auld or Covey, but Frederick still dreamed of freedom. He began teaching other slaves how to read, though he was warned that he should stop. He and other slaves plotted to escape to the

Quick Fact

In the Baltimore shipyards, Frederick painted the hulls of ships with tar to make them waterproof.

north. Their plan was discovered, and they were thrown into jail.

Frederick was then sent back to Hugh Auld in Baltimore. Auld hired him out to work in Baltimore's busy shipyards. There, Frederick helped build ships. He was even allowed to keep some of the money he earned.

Frederick used his job in the shipyards to escape from slavery. On September 3, 1838,

Baltimore's harbor was one of the busiest in the United States during Douglass's lifetime. Ships came in for repairs or to deliver goods.

"The Fugitive's Song" was written in honor of Douglass and his work after he published the story of his life in 1845.

he traveled to New York City using identification borrowed from a free black seaman. Soon after, he sent for Anna Murray, a free black woman that he knew from Baltimore.

Frederick and Murray got married and went to live in New Bedford, Massachusetts, where there was a large community of free African Americans. He changed his name to Frederick Douglass. The couple eventually had five children.

The Douglasses soon became involved in the **ABOLITIONIST MOVEMENT**. They

Vocabulary

The ABOLITIONIST MOVEMENT was an effort to abolish, or end, the practice of slavery. Followers of the movement were known as abolitionists.

Abolitionist William Lloyd Garrison speaks out against slavery in front of a large crowd in Boston. Garrison founded the American Anti-Slavery Society in 1833.

went to antislavery meetings and read antislavery newspapers.

In 1841, Douglass gave a speech at an antislavery convention. He described what his life had been like when he was a slave. Many people in the audience were moved by the speech. A famous abolitionist named William Lloyd Garrison encouraged Douglass to tell his story at more meetings.

CHAPTER FOUR

ABOLITIONIST, WRITER, AND FIGHTER

Douglass became an agent of the Massachusetts Anti-Slavery Society. He started giving speeches to large groups of people. Soon he was one of the abolitionist movement's most famous leaders. Douglass was a powerful speaker. He addressed groups in many northern states, where slavery was illegal.

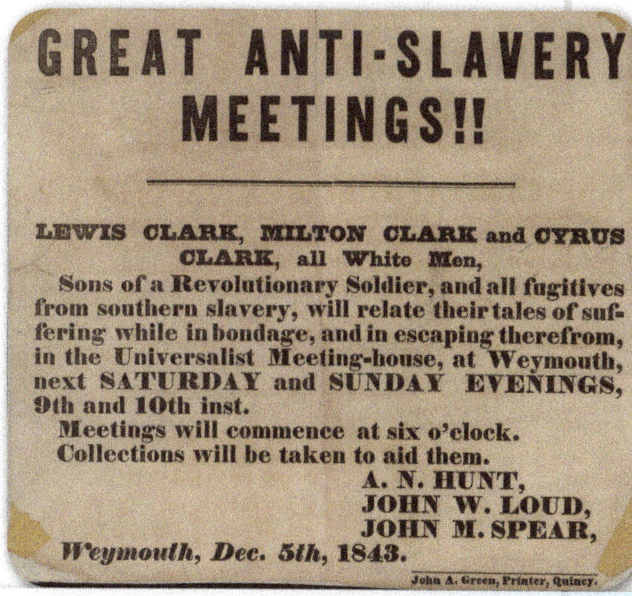

GREAT ANTI-SLAVERY MEETINGS!!

LEWIS CLARK, MILTON CLARK and CYRUS CLARK, all White Men,
Sons of a Revolutionary Soldier, and all fugitives from southern slavery, will relate their tales of suffering while in bondage, and in escaping therefrom, in the Universalist Meeting-house, at Weymouth, next SATURDAY and SUNDAY EVENINGS, 9th and 10th inst.
Meetings will commence at six o'clock.
Collections will be taken to aid them.

A. N. HUNT,
JOHN W. LOUD,
JOHN M. SPEAR,

Weymouth, Dec. 5th, 1843.

John A. Green, Printer, Quincy.

Speeches about the horrors of slavery were a common feature of meetings by abolitionist groups like the Massachusetts Anti-Slavery Society.

Vocabulary

To be DISCRIMINATED against means to be treated unfairly.

Douglass became tired of simply telling the story of his life in slavery. He worked against laws that **DISCRIMINATED** against African Americans. He also traveled through the East and Midwest to speak to antislavery conferences.

Sometimes he was attacked or mocked for speaking. At other times, the people he talked to did not believe that he had even been a slave. They thought that he spoke and dressed too well to have been born into slavery.

Douglass decided to write a book that would prove to people that he had personally experienced slavery. Garrison helped him publish the book, which was called *The Narrative of the Life of Frederick Douglass, an American Slave*. The book told the story of Douglass's years in slavery and of his escape. It was first printed in 1845.

The publication of *The Narrative of the Life of Frederick Douglass, an American Slave* in 1845 made Douglass a very famous man. The book helped inspire people to join the abolitionist movement.

The book was very popular. Many people learned about the mistreatment that Douglass and other slaves faced. However, the book put Douglass in danger. He worried that someone might try to capture him and return him to slavery.

Douglass left the United States in 1845 and traveled to Great Britain. He raised money for abolitionist groups by giving speeches. He talked to large groups of people in Ireland and Great Britain about slavery in the United States. He was a very popular speaker there.

Douglass's fans in Great Britain did not want him to be captured by slave hunters. They raised money for him to buy his freedom from his former owners. Though he had been free since his escape, he was then legally free and no longer had to be afraid of capture.

Douglass returned to the United States in 1847. He and his family moved to the city of Rochester, New York. He founded an abolitionist newspaper there called *The North Star*. The newspaper became successful. He later changed its name to *Frederick Douglass's Paper*. His family helped him publish the paper.

Douglass became the leader of the Underground Railroad in Rochester. The Underground Railroad was a secret network that helped escaped slaves reach places of safety in the North and in Canada.

Douglass became more outspoken on equality issues. He worked to end **SEGREGATION** in Rochester's schools. He wanted African American children to learn trades that would help them become skilled craftspeople.

He also became involved in the women's rights movement. At the time, women in the United States were not allowed to vote. Douglass believed it would be wrong for men who had been slaves to have certain rights if women did not have the same rights. He went to the Seneca Falls Convention in 1848. The convention was a gathering of people who wanted women to have the right to vote.

Douglass's antislavery work continued. He split from William Lloyd Garrison in 1853. Garrison believed that African

> **Vocabulary**
>
> **SEGREGATION** is the forced separation of races, religions, or classes.

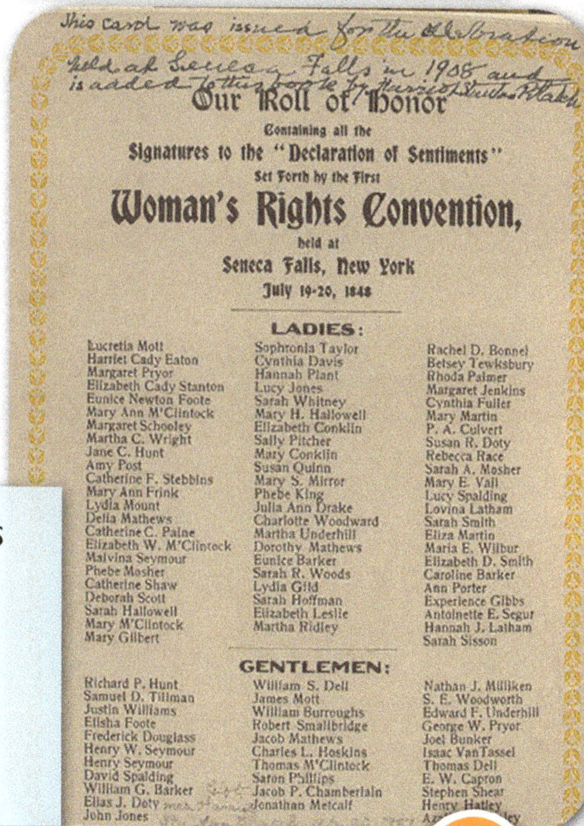

Our Roll of Honor

Containing all the

Signatures to the "Declaration of Sentiments"

Set Forth by the First

Woman's Rights Convention,

held at

Seneca Falls, New York

July 19-20, 1848

LADIES:

Lucretia Mott
Harriet Cady Eaton
Margaret Pryor
Elizabeth Cady Stanton
Eunice Newton Foote
Mary Ann M'Clintock
Margaret Schooley
Martha C. Wright
Jane C. Hunt
Amy Post
Catherine F. Stebbins
Mary Ann Frink
Lydia Mount
Delia Mathews
Catherine C. Paine
Elizabeth W. M'Clintock
Malvina Seymour
Phebe Mosher
Catherine Shaw
Deborah Scott
Sarah Hallowell
Mary M'Clintock
Mary Gilbert
Sophronia Taylor
Cynthia Davis
Hannah Plant
Lucy Jones
Sarah Whitney
Mary H. Hallowell
Elizabeth Conklin
Sally Pitcher
Mary Conklin
Susan Quinn
Mary S. Mirror
Phebe King
Julia Ann Drake
Charlotte Woodward
Martha Underhill
Dorothy Mathews
Eunice Barker
Sarah R. Woods
Lydia Gild
Sarah Hoffman
Elizabeth Leslie
Martha Ridley
Rachel D. Bonnel
Betsey Tewksbury
Rhoda Palmer
Margaret Jenkins
Cynthia Fuller
Mary Martin
P. A. Culvert
Susan R. Doty
Rebecca Race
Sarah A. Mosher
Mary E. Vail
Lucy Spalding
Lovina Latham
Sarah Smith
Eliza Martin
Maria E. Wilbur
Elizabeth D. Smith
Caroline Barker
Ann Porter
Experience Gibbs
Antoinette E. Segur
Hannah J. Latham
Sarah Sisson

GENTLEMEN:

Richard P. Hunt
Samuel D. Tillman
Justin Williams
Elisha Foote
Frederick Douglass
Henry W. Seymour
Henry Seymour
David Spalding
William G. Barker
Elias J. Doty
John Jones
William S. Dell
James Mott
William Burroughs
Robert Smallbridge
Jacob Mathews
Charles L. Hoskins
Thomas M'Clintock
Saron Phillips
Jacob P. Chamberlain
Jonathan Metcalf
Nathan J. Milliken
S. E. Woodworth
Edward F. Underhill
George W. Pryor
Joel Bunker
Isaac VanTassel
Thomas Dell
E. W. Capron
Stephen Shear
Henry Hatley

The Declaration of Sentiments outlined the rights that women should have as citizens. It was put together at the Seneca Falls Convention in New York, held in July 1848. Sixty-eight women and thirty-two men, including Douglass, signed the Declaration of Sentiments.

Quick Fact

Douglass was the only African American to attend the Seneca Falls Convention.

Americans did not have the ability to lead the abolitionist movement.

Douglass supported Abraham Lincoln's 1860 presidential campaign. He met with Lincoln during the American Civil War. In 1863, Douglass was able to talk Lincoln into letting free African Americans fight on the Union side. Douglass raised two units of African American soldiers himself.

Douglass met with President Abraham Lincoln and the president's advisers at the White House. Douglass argued that free African Americans should be allowed to fight in the American Civil War.

CHAPTER FIVE

WORKING FOR EQUALITY

Frederick Douglass was the most famous African American in the United States by the time the Civil War ended in 1865. He was well known for his speaking tours and his newspapers. He had even met with President Lincoln. After the war ended, Douglass kept working for equal rights for everyone.

Douglass had urged Lincoln to free all people living in slavery in the United States. Lincoln did so by working to change the United States Constitution. The Thirteenth **AMENDMENT** to the Constitution was

Vocabulary

An AMENDMENT is a change in the wording or meaning of a law or a document, a written or printed paper.

Huge crowds celebrated in Washington, DC, when the Thirteenth Amendment became law, finally making slavery illegal throughout the United States.

passed in 1865. It officially ended slavery in the United States.

The United States Congress passed the Fifteenth Amendment in 1870. The amendment guaranteed that men of all races could have the right to vote. However, those rights were taken away in many places. Douglass wanted guarantees that their voting rights would be protected. He also urged the government to give land to former slaves.

Douglass continued to support women's right to vote as well. The Equal Rights Party chose him to run for vice president of the United States in the election of 1872. A woman named Victoria Woodhull ran for president. Douglass was chosen without his knowledge and did not campaign. Still, he was the first African American to be picked as a vice-presidential running mate.

Douglass is shown at the top of this picture that marks the passing of the Fifteenth Amendment in 1870. He appears between Army Major Martin Delany and Senator Hiram Rhoades Revels of Mississippi.

Douglass held several important government positions after the Civil War. He was appointed as a member of the law-making council of Washington, DC, in 1871.

Quick Fact

Douglass was the first African American to be approved for a government post by the United States Senate.

He took on another responsibility when he became president of the Freedman's Bank, which served former slaves, in 1874. Other official work followed. He was appointed to serve as a United States marshal for Washington in 1877. He became the city's recorder of deeds in 1881.

Douglass was also appointed to serve as the United States' foreign minister to Haiti. This meant that he represented the US government in dealings with the government of Haiti. He was the first African American to serve as a foreign minister. He held this post from 1889 to 1891.

Visitors to the Frederick Douglass House in Washington, DC, can see the room where Douglass worked during the final years of his life.

Douglass spent his final years living in Washington, DC. He continued to travel for his work. His wife, Anna, died in 1882. He married a white woman named Helen Pitts in 1884. Marriages between people of different races were very rare at the time.

Douglass stayed very busy. He handled his government jobs and kept writing. He also continued to publish newspapers. He remained a popular speaker, even after slavery ended. He died on February 20, 1895, after attending a conference on women's right to vote.

Nine-year-old Ahriana Merryweather shows off her award for winning a public speaking contest held at the Frederick Douglass House on his 194th birthday.

Vocabulary

The CIVIL RIGHTS MOVEMENT refers to the struggle to gain equal rights for African Americans, especially through a series of protests and other events in the 1950s and 1960s.

Today, Douglass is seen as one of the greatest speakers of the nineteenth century. He influenced many people through his speeches, his newspapers, and his writings. He spent his life working for freedom and equal rights for all people. Douglass's words inspired countless leaders of the **CIVIL RIGHTS MOVEMENT** who came after him. They still have the power to inspire people today.

TIMELINE

1818: Frederick Douglass is born into slavery in Talbot County, Maryland, as Frederick Augustus Washington Bailey.

1826: Douglass works as a slave in the home of Hugh Auld in Baltimore.

1832: Hugh Auld sends Douglass to the plantation belonging to his brother.

1834: Douglass begins to work for William Freeland.

1835: Douglass plots to escape with other slaves. The plan is discovered, and they are jailed.

1838: Hugh Auld hires Douglass out to work in Baltimore's shipyards. Douglass escapes to New York City.

1841: Douglass gives his first public speech about his life in slavery.

1845: Douglass publishes *Narrative of the Life of Frederick Douglass, an American Slave* and travels to Europe to speak about slavery.

1847: Douglass returns to the United States and buys his freedom. He starts an abolitionist newspaper, *The North Star*.

1848: Douglass attends the Seneca Falls Convention.

1863: Douglass convinces President Abraham Lincoln to allow African Americans to fight in the American Civil War.

1865: The Thirteenth Amendment to the US Constitution is passed.

1870: The Fifteenth Amendment to the US Constitution is passed.

1877: Douglass is appointed to serve as a US marshal in Washington, DC.

1881: Douglass becomes recorder of deeds in Washington, DC.

1889: Douglass is appointed to serve as foreign minister to Haiti.

1895: Douglass dies in Washington, DC, on February 20.

GLOSSARY

ANTISLAVERY Opposing slavery.

APPOINT To choose for some job or office.

CAMPAIGN A series of activities through which a candidate for an office tries to convince voters that he or she is right for the job.

COMMUNITY A group of people with common interests, especially when living together.

CONGRESS The chief lawmaking body of the United States, made up of the Senate and the House of Representatives.

CONVENTION A meeting of people for a common purpose.

CRAFTSPEOPLE Workers who practice a trade or craft.

EQUALITY The fact or state of being equal.

GUARANTEE To promise that some condition holds or will be fulfilled.

INFLUENCE To affect or change in an indirect but usually important way.

INSPIRE To make someone want to do something.

MARSHAL A federal official having duties similar to those of a sheriff.

MOCK To laugh at or make fun of someone.

NETWORK A group or system of related or connected parts.

PUBLISH To prepare and print a book, newspaper, or other work for sale.

SLAVE HUNTER A person who captures and returns runaway slaves to their owners.

SLAVERY The practice of people owning other people.

TRADE The business or work in which a person takes part regularly.

BOOKS

Lassieur, Allison. *The Underground Railroad: An Interactive History Adventure.* Rev. ed. North Mankato, MN: Capstone Press, 2016.

Myers, Walter Dean. *Frederick Douglass: The Lion Who Wrote History.* New York, NY: HarperCollins, 2017.

Rappaport, Doreen. *Frederick's Journey: The Life of Frederick Douglass.* Los Angeles, CA: Disney/Hyperion, 2016.

Shaffer, Jody Jensen. *What's Your Story, Frederick Douglass?* (Cub Reporter Meets Famous Americans). Minneapolis, MN: Lerner Publications, 2016.

WEBSITES

Because of the changing nature of internet links, Rosen Publishing has developed an online list of websites related to the subject of this book. This site is updated regularly. Please use this link to access the list:

http://www.rosenlinks.com/BBB/Douglass

INDEX